Day and Night

Words by
David Bennett

Pictures by
Rosalinda Kightley

In the day, the sun is in the sky.
The sun makes our world light and warm.

At night, after the sun has set, it is dark.
You may see the moon shining
and the stars twinkling in the sky.

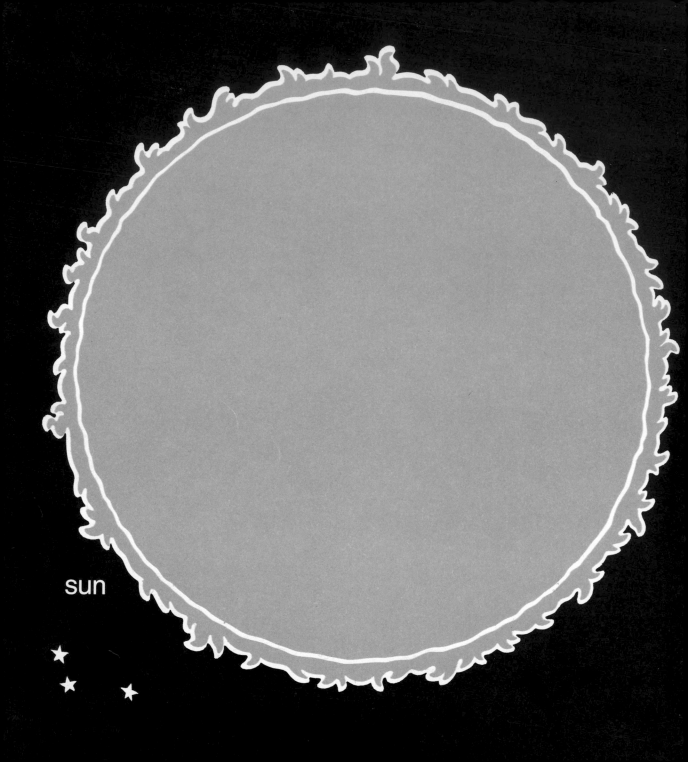

sun

Our world is a planet called Earth. It floats in space with other planets and the sun and the moon. The sun is much bigger than the earth. The moon is much smaller.

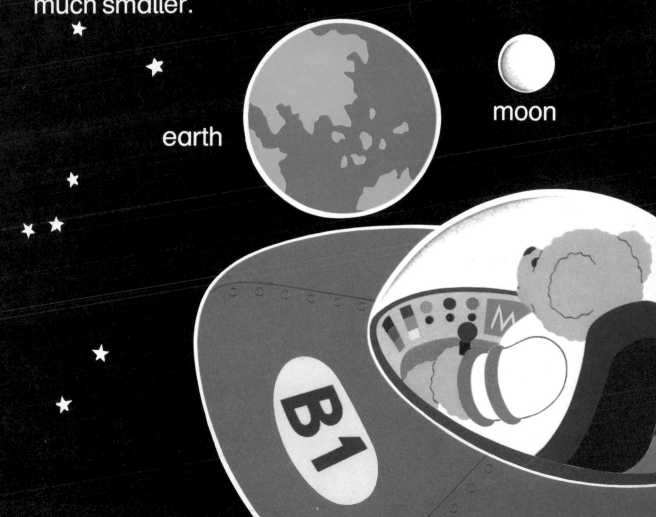

earth

moon

B1

The sun is one of the millions of stars in the sky. It looks much bigger than the other stars because it is closer to us.

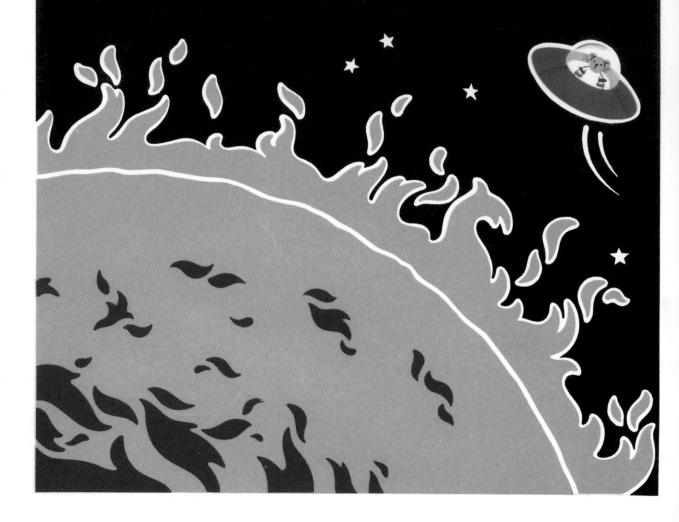

We see the moon at night. It looks quiet and calm. There is no life on the moon because there is no air to breathe or water to drink.

The earth turns round and round all the time.
It takes a whole day and night to turn round once.
When your part of the earth turns to face the sun,
it is day.

On the other side of the earth it is night.
The people who live there are going to sleep
when you are waking up in the morning.

Sunrise means the beginning of a new day.
The sun seems to be moving up into the sky.
But the sun does not move.
It only looks that way because the earth is
turning round and round.

The earth keeps turning and, by the middle of the day, the sun looks very high in the sky. This is the hottest and brightest time of day.

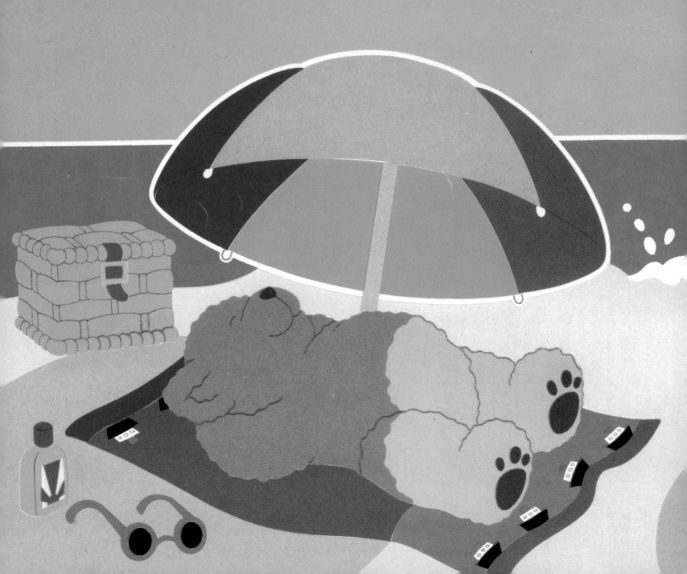

In some places, it gets so hot that people and other animals have to stay out of the sun.

After the middle of the day, your part of the earth begins to turn away from the sun.
The sun looks lower in the sky.
The sky is not as bright, and the air is cooler.

At the end of the day, your part of the earth turns further away from the sun. Day turns into evening.

At sunset, the sun disappears from view,
and the sky changes colour — sometimes
it turns orange and red and even pink.

Without light and warmth from the sun,
it becomes dark and cool outside.
It is night. Your part of the earth has
turned away from the sun.

We can make our own light and warmth.

Do you know how?

Even though you cannot see the sun at night, its light still reaches the moon and other parts of the earth.

The sun's light makes the moon shine in the sky. Stars make their own light. But the moon has no light of its own.

On some nights, the moon looks a different shape. The whole moon is always there, but sometimes we can only see part of it.

At night, it is time to go to sleep.
But some animals, such as bats and owls,
are wide-awake. They sleep during the day.

During the night, the earth keeps turning.
On the other side of the earth it is day.

What happens next?
Soon your part of the world is facing the
sun again. As the sun appears in the
sky, a new day begins.

Do you know what is happening on the other side of the earth?

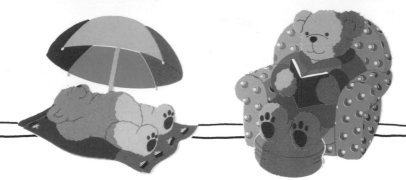

BEAR REVIEW

1. The earth is always turning. The sun does not move.

2. When your part of the earth is facing the sun, it is day.

3. When your part of the earth turns away from the sun, it is night.

4. The people who live on the other side of the earth are going to sleep when you are waking up in the morning.